STEPHEN COLBERT'S

MIDNIGHT CONFESSIONS

BY THE STAFF OF THE LATE SHOW WITH STEPHEN COLBERT

ILLUSTRATIONS BY SEAN KELLY

SIMON & SCHUSTER

NEW YORK LONDON TORONTO SYDNEY NEW DELHI

Simon & Schuster
1230 Avenue of the Americas
New York, NY 10020

First Simon & Schuster hardcover edition September 2017

SIMON & SCHUSTER and colophon are registered trademarks of Simon & Schuster, Inc.

For information about special discounts for bulk purchases, please contact Simon & Schuster
Special Sales at 1-866-506-1949 or business@simonandschuster.com

The Simon & Schuster Speakers Bureau can bring authors to your live event. For more information or to book an event,
contact the Simon & Schuster Speakers Bureau at 1-866-248-3049 or visit our website at www.simonspeakers.com.

Interior design and illustrations by Sean Kelly

Manufactured in the United States of America

1   3   5   7   9   10   8   6   4   2

Library of Congress Cataloging-in-Publication Data is available.

ISBN 978-1-5011-6900-7
ISBN 978-1-5011-6901-4 (ebook)

To human frailty.
If you have no regrets, I don't want to know you.

BLESS ME, READERS, FOR I HAVE PUBLISHED.

IT'S BEEN FIVE YEARS SINCE MY LAST BOOK.

reetings, fellow sinners! If you picked up a copy of this book, it means you are either: 1) wracked with guilt and are looking for penance, or 2) need to spend over $10.00 at the airport newsstand so you can use your credit card. Either way, welcome to *Stephen Colbert's Midnight Confessions.*

As America's foremost TV Catholic, it was natural for me to do a segment inspired by the church. After all, the Catholic Church and late-night TV actually have a lot in common: our shows last about an hour, we're obsessed with reaching younger demographics, and the hosts are almost always men.

This religious-adjacent tome contains all my favorite confessions from *The Late Show*. These are things that aren't necessarily sins, but I do feel guilty about them. For instance, repackaging material from the show and selling it in a book.

I've always been a big fan of confession. The confessional is a great place to go to relieve yourself of your sins. Unless you're claustrophobic, in which case it's a suffocating death trap of despair!

And while most confession books just give you run-of-the-mill mortal sins, I go one step further and provide you with mortal sins, venial sins, deadly sins, and even sins of omission

(Notice that the previous sentence didn't have a period!)

This book is a throwback to a simpler time when people would go to a priest to confess their sins. As opposed to how it's done now—getting drunk and weeping to Andy Cohen on Bravo.

Confessing your sins is a great way to get things off your chest. Second only to waxing.

The only downside is that you get introduced to it as a kid, before you have any juicy sins to confess. Oh, you stole a cookie? That's adorable, Becky. Come back when you total your dad's Chevy.

Now you might be asking yourself, "What if I'm not Catholic—can I still enjoy this book?" Of course. After all, no matter what religion you are—be it Jewish, Muslim, Lutheran, Pagan, or SoulCycle—we all have things to feel guilty about. For example, not being Catholic.

If you're not familiar with confession, think of the priest as God's police officer. If you confess to him, he'll cut you a deal that gets you out of hell earlier, and if you snitch on your fellow sinners, you get a plush new identity in heaven's witness protection program. Pretty sure that's how it works.

And it wouldn't be a book of confessions if I didn't begin by me getting a few things I feel guilty about off my chest:

- *When I put together this book, I asked God for inspiration. When that didn't work, I used a large font and wide margins.*

- *To this day, I still can't tell my publishers, Simon & Schuster, apart.*

- *Confession wasn't my first choice of sacrament to turn into a late-night bit. But CBS wouldn't let me build a baptismal font on stage.*

- *I've never actually read the entire Bible. I skimmed the Old Testament and figured out the rest by watching* Godspell.

- *Sometimes during confession I get worried the priest is bored so I just start describing episodes of* Breaking Bad.

- *And when I've run out of things to confess, I just look around the confessional booth for ideas. That's why numerous times I've confessed to being aroused by wood paneling.*

But, truth be told, this book doesn't contain just my confessions. It also includes confessions from the viewing public. I opened up it up to people on Twitter, and @jesuschrist, there are a lot of troubled people on there.

Which reminds me, I have one more confession:

- *I will not be paying any of those people on Twitter for their confessions.*

In conclusion, I just want to thank the Catholic Church for inventing confession, and my parish priest for never mentioning that I do this segment.

So there you have it. With any luck, this book will be an even better seller than the Bible! Sorry, God, but all is fair in publishing.

Oh, and if for some reason you're just perusing this book in the airport newsstand instead of buying it, I forgive you.

For penance, simply say ten Hail Marys, twenty Our Fathers, and purchase forty copies of this book.

STEPHEN COLBERT

STEPHEN COLBERT'S

MIDNIGHT CONFESSIONS

STANDARD DISCLAIMER:

I don't know
if these are
technically sins,
but I do feel bad
about them.

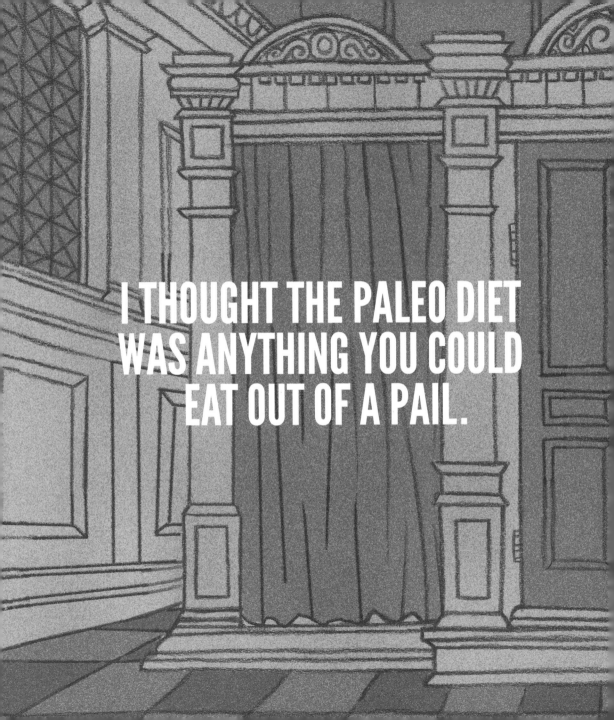

I don't stretch before I exercise . . .

. . . because I don't exercise.

WHEN I WAS IN COLLEGE, I CHEATED IN PSYCHOLOGY,

SO I'LL NEVER KNOW WHAT THAT SAYS ABOUT ME.

People
say I have
a gambling
problem,
but I bet I don't.

I'M A MAN IN HIS FIFTIES WHO EATS LIKE A MAN IN HIS TWENTIES WHO DOESN'T PLAN TO MAKE IT TO HIS THIRTIES.

WHATEVER IT IS, I THINK IF I IGNORE IT, IT WILL GO AWAY.

IF I TELL YOU
I'M STUCK
IN TRAFFIC,
IT MEANS
I HAVEN'T
LEFT YET.

CBS: THE LATE SHOW WITH STEPHEN COLBERT

OPENING MONOLOGUE

STEPHEN:

I take credit for other people's work. And if I had writers, they'd be pretty pissed.

WHEN I GO INTO
A MCDONALD'S
THAT HAS THE
CALORIES
PRINTED ON
THE MENU . . .

. . . I PRETEND
THEY'RE POINTS
AND I'M
GOING TO WIN.

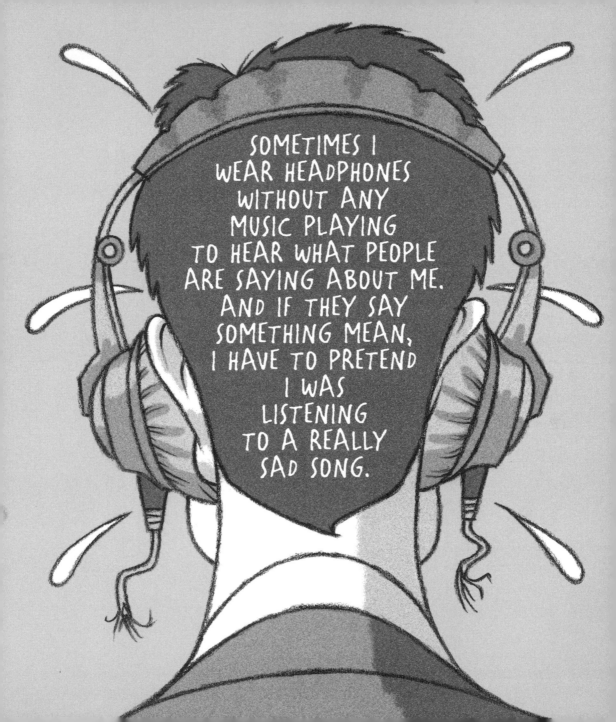

I HAVE VIOLENT THOUGHTS WHEN PEOPLE USE THE TERMS "SCI-FI" AND "FANTASY" INTERCHANGEABLY.

"OH, I LOVE SCIENCE FICTION. I JUST READ LORD OF THE RINGS."

I WILL END YOU.

IF I'M REALLY HONEST WITH MYSELF . . .

. . . I'M NEVER QUITE READY FOR SOME FOOTBALL.

I'M A
FIFTY-ONE-
YEAR-OLD MAN,
BUT I CAN NAME
EVERY MEMBER OF
TAYLOR SWIFT'S
GIRL SQUAD.

I give to
the homeless
only when I'm
trying to get
rid of pennies.

I KIND OF LIKE
YANKEE CANDLE.

WHEN I CLICK ON A HEADLINE THAT SAYS ANOTHER SPECIES HAS GONE EXTINCT, I'M SAD.

BUT I ALSO WONDER IF IT TASTED GOOD.

TONIGHT'S ENTREES

Roasted Pinta Island Tortoise

o

Yangtze River Dolphin au jus

o

Blackened Bermuda Hawk

o

Pan-Seared Madagascan
Dwarf Hippopotamus

o

I floss my teeth only twice a year...

...when the dentist does it for me.

EVERY
YEAR,
I GO
ON MY
WIKIPEDIA
PAGE
AND MAKE
MYSELF
ONE INCH TALLER.

I NEVER PITCH IN
FOR PIZZA.

BUT I ALWAYS
TAKE THE LAST SLICE.

OLIVE GARDEN OFFERS
"UNLIMITED BREADSTICKS,"
BUT OVER THE
CHRISTMAS BREAK . . .
I FOUND THEIR LIMIT.

My dog
isn't really
a service dog.
I just bought him
a vest online
so I could take him
to the movies
with me.

SOMETIMES I LOOK AT A SHAMPOO BOTTLE AND THINK, "SHOULDN'T THEY HAVE TESTED THIS ON ANIMALS FIRST?"

OTHERWISE, AREN'T THEY TESTING IT ON ME?

I wish there was
an app that
made me forget
where my iPhone
was made.

I LIKE
THE Y
BECAUSE
WORKING OUT
NEXT TO
THE ELDERLY
MAKES ME
FEEL FIT.

I HAVE
TROUBLE
GETTING
MAD ABOUT
WOODROW WILSON
BEING RACIST
WHEN MOST OF
MY MONEY
HAS SLAVE
OWNERS
ON IT.

*I update my iPhone software
way more often than
I call my sister.*

WHEN PEOPLE GET DIVORCED . . .

. . . I <u>DO</u> BLAME THE KIDS.

I take hotel
shampoo bottles.

Even when
I'm not staying
at the hotel.

Yesterday I told a coworker she had the cutest baby. But really it was more of a 6.

I have a fair amount of gay friends, but sometimes . . .

. . . I worry that I haven't made enough gay enemies.

I'M NOT ON
FACEBOOK,
BUT IF I WAS, 'T
I STILL WOULDN'T
CARE ABOUT
YOUR TRIP
TO ITALY.

I HAVE IMPURE THOUGHTS ABOUT THE LAND O'LAKES BUTTER LADY.

BUT MOSTLY ABOUT THE BUTTER.

IF THERE'S
NO HEAVEN,
I WILL RISE
FROM THE
DEAD AND
GHOST-PUNCH
THE POPE.

Sometimes when I'm out to dinner with my wife, I'll propose so we'll get free dessert.

Sometimes I lie awake at night, afraid I'll die before I get to use all my forever stamps.

I told my staff
I was late for work
because I was
stuck in traffic.
But actually,
I don't know
what time
work starts.

I don't understand why it's not called a "pants suit" when a man wears it.

SOMETIMES WHEN I GO
TO A GARAGE SALE,
I SNEAK IN SOME OF
MY OWN JUNK
AND RUN.

I SAW SOMETHING,
SO I SAID SOMETHING.

BUT THE THING I SAID . . . WASN'T THE THING I SAW.

REMEMBER THAT FUNNY

VIRAL VIDEO YOU SENT ME?

I DIDN'T WATCH IT.

I JUST WAITED FIVE MINUTES

AND TEXTED "LOL."

I once waited nine hours to reply to a text and then said, "Oops, I just saw this now. I hope you were able to find someone to pick up your kid from pre-K."

IF YOU'VE EVER
WALKED SLOWLY
IN FRONT OF ME
ON THE SIDEWALK,
I'VE FANTASIZED
ABOUT
KILLING YOU.

I steal office supplies.
From Staples.

THEY ALWAYS SAY
"IF YOU LOVE SOMETHING, SET IT FREE."

BUT I DON'T KNOW IF I CAN
REALLY TRUST THOSE PEOPLE
I'VE GOT IN MY SHED.

I'm
terrible
at keeping
secrets.

ONE TIME
IN A STORE,
I USED THE
EMPLOYEES ONLY
BATHROOM BY
TELLING THEM I
WAS A REGIONAL
MANAGER.

I've never joined the Mile-High Club, but I _am_ in the Greyhound Bus Terminal Utility Closet Guild.

I blame
my farts
on the dog.

Also my
tax evasion.

If I'm nervous
speaking to a
group of people,
I picture them
naked.
And if I'm
really nervous,
I photograph
them naked.

I WEAR SUNGLASSES ON THE SUBWAY SO NO ONE SEES ME PEEKING AT THEIR TEXT MESSAGES.

ACTUALLY, I LIED. I DON'T RIDE THE SUBWAY.

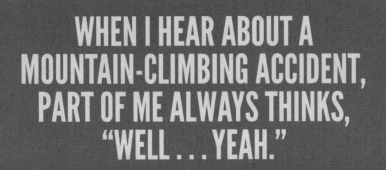

WHEN I HEAR ABOUT A
MOUNTAIN-CLIMBING ACCIDENT,
PART OF ME ALWAYS THINKS,
"WELL . . . YEAH."

I TELL
PEOPLE I'M
CLAUSTROPHOBIC
JUST SO
I CAN
SCREAM IN
ELEVATORS.

I wouldn't
hurt a fly.

But when it comes
to mosquitoes,
I am one sick son
of a bitch.

I HAVEN'T
LOOKED IN MY
REFRIGERATOR'S
CRISPER
SINCE 1987.

I CAN HEAR
THE BRUSSELS
SPROUTS
SCREAMING.

One time I saw a lion attack a warthog in a nature documentary, and I whispered, "Hakuna matata, bitch."

I tell my kids never to use swear words, even though they learned them all from me.

When I go to real confession at church, I disguise my voice to sound like Gregory Peck.

Sometimes I wish
I had more health
problems, because
the people in
pharmaceutical ads
have more picnics
than I do.

I HAVE
NO
SKELETONS
IN
MY
CLOSET.

THEY'RE BURIED UNDER THE PORCH.

IF I SNEEZE
AND SOMEBODY
DOESN'T SAY
"BLESS YOU,"
I AIM THE
NEXT SNEEZE
TOWARD THEM.

One of my biggest fears is eating something really healthy just before I die.

I ONCE
BURNED A BOAT
JUST TO COLLECT
THE INSURANCE
MONEY.

AND ONLY
LATER
REMEMBERED
THAT I DON'T
OWN A BOAT.

I did terrible things to rise to the top of my barbershop quartet.

I DON'T KNOW
HOW TO TELL IF
AN AVOCADO IS RIPE.

I JUST SQUEEZE THREE
AND THEN BUY
THE SECOND ONE.

I haven't finished
a book in twenty years.

Don't tell me how
the Bible ends.
I think Jesus is
gonna pull
this one out.

WHENEVER I SEE A BOWL OF M&M'S AT A PARTY, I ALWAYS TOSS IN A COUPLE SKITTLES JUST TO FREAK PEOPLE OUT.

I actually enjoy nightmares about being naked in the middle of a high school test, because back then I was in a lot better shape.

I GAVE MY KIDS A QUARTER EVERY TIME THEY LOST A BABY TOOTH, BUT I WAS SELLING THEM FOR WAY MORE THAN THAT.

I HAVE NEVER
CLEANED MY OVEN.

I JUST MOVE EVERY
FEW YEARS.

As you know,
I am a practicing
Catholic.

Unfortunately, I
don't make it to
church as often
as I used to
because I feel like
my Sundays are
kind of sacred.

One of the wise
men in my
Nativity scene
broke, and
instead of buying
a new one,
I replaced him
with Lego Batman.

When my kids were growing up, our house didn't have a fireplace. So I told them that Santa came out of the dryer.

I'M A SLOW TYPER
BECAUSE I USE ONLY
TWO FINGERS.

AND THEY'RE NOT MINE.

Last night, I lost over a pint of blood because I flossed for the first time in two years.

I read

erotic fan fiction,

but I write

erotic fan nonfiction.

I DON'T SMOKE,
BUT SOMETIMES
I DRAMATICALLY
THROW A PACK OF
CIGARETTES OFF A
BRIDGE TO MAKE
PEOPLE THINK
I JUST QUIT.

I have
no idea
how the
stock market
works,
and all my
money is in it.

WHENEVER IT LOOKS LIKE I'M TAKING NOTES IN A MEETING, I'M JUST DRAWING KING KONG FIGHTING TANKS.

WHEN I'M AT KARAOKE AND SOMEONE STARTS SINGING "DON'T STOP BELIEVIN' "...

I STOP BELIEVIN'.

I ALWAYS THOUGHT
MY MOST SATISFYING
EXPERIENCE WOULD
BE FATHERHOOD, BUT
ACTUALLY IT'S EATING
YOGURT PRETZELS, DRUNK.

Sometimes I stare into the distance to seem thoughtful. But I'm really just trying to make a bird outside the window explode with my mind.

I think riding
a roller coaster is
the most fun thing
in the world.
Then again,
I've never
tried crack.

One time
a little kid asked me
if famous people like me
go to the bathroom.

I lied and
told him yes.

I DIDN'T KNOW
THERE WASN'T A
DIFFERENCE
BETWEEN
"FLAMMABLE" AND
"INFLAMMABLE"...

. . . WHICH IS WHY
THE JUDGE TAUGHT
ME THE DIFFERENCE
BETWEEN GUILTY
AND NOT GUILTY.

When the treadmill
asks me to enter
my weight, I do—
from that one time
I had mono in college.

BED, BATH, AND BEYOND

ARE MY THREE FAVORITE

LOCATIONS TO HAVE SEX.

I DON'T SAY
"SPOILER ALERT"
BEFORE GIVING AWAY
THE ENDING TO
A MOVIE.

OR SERVING
BAD CLAMS.

When people say "God gives you only as much as you can handle," I wonder if they could handle getting punched in the face.

I never bring anything
to potlucks, but I
always leave with, like,
a handful of batteries.

I NEVER GO TO THE GYM.

SO I BOUGHT A HOME GYM.

NOW I NEVER GO HOME.

I can still name all
four of the Teletubbies.
And have done so
in my will.

Sometimes
when I
wake up
from a
beautiful
dream,
I feel a little sad . . .
when I see
the car
I just rear-ended.

I DON'T ALWAYS
DRINK BEER.

BUT WHEN I DO,
I MAKE UP FOR ALL
THE TIMES I DON'T.

They say there's no
wrong way to eat
a Reese's, but I'm
thinking a whole bag
while you're idling
in the driveway
is close.

WHENEVER MY
MEDICINE SAYS
TO TAKE IT
ON AN EMPTY
STOMACH,
I NEVER TAKE
IT, BECAUSE
I NEVER HAVE
AN EMPTY
STOMACH.

When I'm in a doctor's office and there are people in the waiting room ahead of me, a little part of me wishes they would die.

I like to lie down while watching TV so I can use my belly button to hold dip.

I NEVER TELL THE
FLIGHT ATTENDANT, BUT I AM
NOT PREPARED TO HELP OUT
IN THE EMERGENCY EXIT ROW.

WHAT AM I SUPPOSED TO DO
WITH THE DOOR AGAIN?
RIDE IT DOWN THE WING
LIKE A SURFBOARD?

I LIKE BEING
AN ADULT,
BUT I WISH
ALL MY SHOES
WERE VELCRO.

Sometimes I go to the bathroom just to check my phone without seeming rude.

I think women look great in stiletto heels, but if I were a woman and a man asked me to wear them, I would murder him with my shoes.

WHEN PEOPLE SAY I'M SELF-CENTERED . . .

. . . I CAN'T HELP BUT THINK THEY'RE TALKING ABOUT ME.

When I was a child,
I had a lot of
imaginary friends.

They were real
people.

I just imagined they
were my friends.

I know
how to fold
fitted sheets,
but I will never
tell my wife.

WHEN I CATCH A FISH,
I ALWAYS THROW IT BACK.

BUT ONLY AFTER STARING
INTO ITS EYES AND SAYING,
"YOU OWE ME ONE."

I really want washboard abs . . .

. . . but all I have is
a fabric-softener ass.

Before I did
my taxes,
I duct-taped
a printer
to my son and
claimed him as
a home office.

I'M JUST GOING TO KEEP POURING BACON GREASE DOWN THE DRAIN UNTIL I HAVE TO MOVE.

I TELL MY FAMILY
THAT WE HAVE
AN EMERGENCY
PREPAREDNESS KIT,
BUT THE ONLY THING
IN THERE IS A CLIF BAR
AND NUNCHUCKS.

SOMETIMES I'LL PET
A DOG JUST BECAUSE
I HAVE SOMETHING GROSS
ON MY HAND THAT
I NEED TO WIPE OFF.

WHEN I GO TO
A BATHROOM AND
SEE ONE OF THOSE

EMPLOYEES MUST
WASH HANDS

SIGNS,
I ALWAYS THINK,
"IT'S A GOOD THING
I DON'T WORK HERE."

AT THE
PETTING ZOO,
INSTEAD OF
FOOD PELLETS,
I FEED THE GOATS
ADDERALL SO
THEY PAY MORE
ATTENTION TO ME.

I THINK INCOME INEQUALITY IS
ONE OF AMERICA'S GREATEST PROBLEMS . . .

. . . UNTIL THEY BRING ME THAT LITTLE HOT TOWEL IN FIRST CLASS.

HAPPY
BIRTHDAY

I HAVE NEVER
FILLED OUT A
BIRTHDAY CARD
ANYWHERE OTHER THAN
IN THE BATHROOM OF
THE RESTAURANT WHERE
WE'RE CELEBRATING
YOUR BIRTHDAY.

YOU KNOW HOW ON AIRPLANES THEY HAVE THAT "SECURE YOUR OXYGEN MASK BEFORE HELPING OTHERS" RULE?

I DON'T NEED TO BE TOLD THAT.

Until I got married, I once went eleven years without changing my sheets.

1985

1987

1990

1993

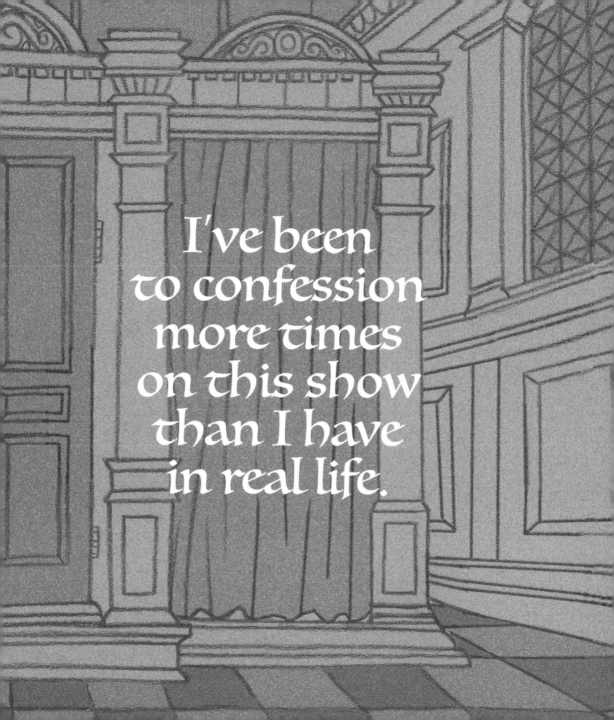

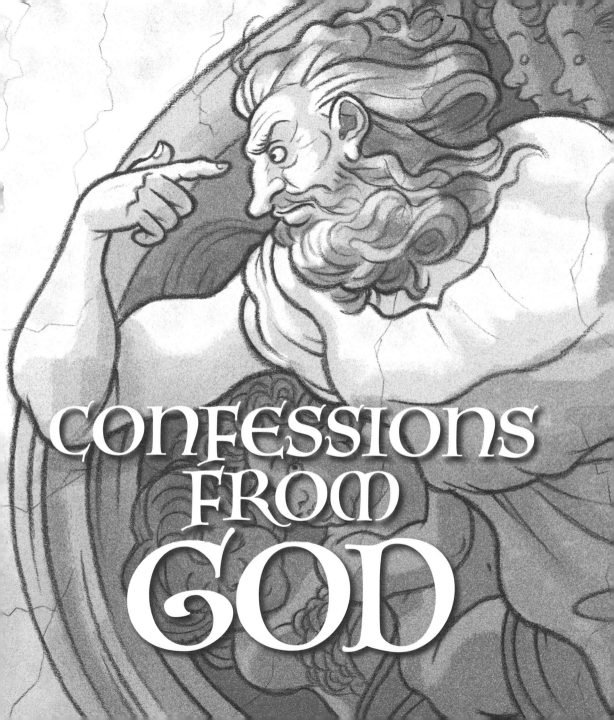

CONFESSIONS FROM GOD

Sometimes when people pray to me, I just nod politely like I'm actually listening.

Last week,
I heard a really
stoned guy say,
"You ever notice
that 'God' spelled
backward is 'dog'?"

And I'll be honest,
it kinda freaked
me out.

I still feel bad that in the 2006 Academy Awards, I let the movie *Crash* win the Oscar over *Brokeback Mountain*.

STEPHEN COLBERT'S
MIDNIGHT CONFESSIONS

TWITTER EDITION

 **Joel Michalak**
@noveltyfriend

Sometimes I fake an orgasm so my roommates don't suspect I'm in my room scrapbooking. #LateShowConfessions

3:41 PM - 7 Apr 2016

 **Andrew Hutchinson**
@FavouriteHutch

@colbertlateshow I get pleasure from finding vegan recipes and then adding meat when I cook them #lateshowconfessions

5:51 PM - 4 May 2016

 **Peter Erickson**
@pjerickson

@ColbertLateShow When I say I already have other plans set in stone, what I really mean is that I plan to go get stoned
#LateShowConfessions

2:33 PM - 12 May 2016

 Bonnie J Heath
@bonheath

I have purposely postponed teaching my son how to read a clock so that I can put him to bed any time I want. #lateshowconfessions

9:21 PM - 1 May 2016

 Peter Erickson
@pjerickson

@colbertlateshow Sometimes I make up words in order to sound more aproserial
#LateShowConfessions

9:11 AM - 6 May 2016

Kevin Baier

@TheKevinBaier

@StephenAtHome I tell people I have herpes, so they won't want to borrow my Chapstick #lateshowconfessions

10:39 PM - 15 Jul 2016

♡ ⟲ ♡ ✉

N8 Burns

@NateRayBurns

When I was 15 I used to hide my porn mags in my step dad's horse stables.Now if I smell hay I think of boobs. #LateShowConfessions

12:29 PM - 16 Jul 2016

♡ ⟲ ♡ ✉

Kathy

@leafsweetie

when asked to "wave your hands in the air like you just don't care", I wave but do care. #LateShowConfessions

3:09 PM - 4 Aug 2016

♡ ⟲ ♡ ✉

Mike OB
@mikeobn

When the kids were little we referred to the ice cream truck as "the music truck" so we didn't have to spend any money.#LateShowConfessions

1:26 PM - 29 Jul 2016

 **Mahatma Ghamdhi**
@HushavPather

I once made brownies and told friends they were weed brownies and watched them get 'high' #LateShowConfessions

2:56 PM - 4 Aug 2016

Adil
@ahussa2

Replying to @colbertlateshow

@colbertlateshow I only donate nickels to the March of Dimes. #lateshowconfessions

4:03 PM - 27 Apr 2016

Braxton
@braxtonryn

I went through a Dunkin Donuts drive thru and started talking to the garbage can instead of the speaker #LateShowConfessions

11:12 AM - 29 Jul 2016

Dustin Pari ✓
@dustinpari

Once a police officer asked if I knew why he pulled me over. I lied and said no... but I knew. #LateShowConfessions

11:42 PM - 7 Apr 2016

 **Taylor Roth**
@Nebraska_Taylor

.@colbertlateshow On days I feel lazy, I shake my FitBit around to reach my step goal for the day. #LateShowConfessions

12:44 PM - 7 Apr 2016

 Mallen 181
@Mallen1811

@colbertlateshow If this tweet counts, I've been to confession twice in my life. #LateShowConfessions

11:51 AM - 7 Apr 2016

 tony dupre
@TheBoneShackles

I've memorized all of the scriptures in the Bible where boobs are mentioned #LateShowConfessions @colbertlateshow

11:49 PM - 6 Apr 2016

Heather Reed
@Hrachelle_21

@colbertlateshow
I've never told anyone
this before, but, I have
no idea how plastic
wrap works
#lateshowconfessions

11:46 PM - 6 Apr 2016

Lando
@LandoThePug

Until the 6th grade I thought lesbians were what you called people who lived in Libya.
#ArkansasEducation #LateShowConfessions

11:47 PM - 6 Apr 2016

Regulos Xavier
@regulos14

I tell people that the book is better than the movie, but I don't even know if the movie has a book. #LateShowConfessions

12:41 AM - 8 Apr 2016

Douglas Spector
@DouglasSpector

@colbertlateshow sometimes I walk my dog at night and just pretend to pick up his poop #LateShowConfessions

7:18 PM - 7 Jun 2016

John Burton
@Beansrdone

Sometimes I eat Jimmy Fallon's ice cream while I watch Stephen Colbert's show. @StephenAtHome #LateShowConfessions

6:43 PM - 17 Jun 2016 from Simpsonville, SC

J.D. Gordon
@jdgordonbooks

I park my smartcar between 2 trucks in the parking lot so drivers think they found an open spot until the last moment #LateShowConfessions

7:59 AM - 20 Jun 2016

Ava
@AvaTheAvian

Sometimes I think to myself "I know you're listening" just in case someone can read my mind. #LateShowConfessions

8:34 PM - 18 Jun 2016

Lauren Vaughan
@MeLaurenVaughan

Whenever my cats meow at me, I always answer, "I know!" But it's a lie. I don't know. I don't have a clue. #LateShowConfessions

10:37 PM - 18 Jun 2016

Andrew DiMola
@AndrewDiMola

#MidnightConfessions @colbertlateshow
I buy party-sized bags of Tostitos, but I only invite myself to the party.

2:49 PM - 2 Nov 2016

YOUR CONFESSIONS

AFTER FILLING THESE PAGES WITH YOUR DARKEST SECRETS, BURN THIS BOOK.
THEN BUY ANOTHER COPY.

ACKNOWLEDGMENTS

Mike Brumm, Nate Charny, Aaron Cohen, Stephen Colbert, Cullen Crawford, Paul Dinello, Ariel Dumas, Glenn Eichler, Django Gold, Gabe Gronli, Barry Julien, Jay Katsir, Daniel Kibblesmith, James Kuo, Matt Lappin, Chris Licht, Bill Marko, Opus Moreschi, Michael Pielocik, Tom Purcell, Greg Reutershan, Kate Sidley, Jen Spyra, Brian Stack, John Thibodeaux, Jon Karp, Eloy Bleifuss, Jackie Seow, Sean Kelly, Jonathan Evans, Kayley Hoffman, Ruth Lee-Mui, Cary Goldstein, Stephen Bedford, Emily Graff, Stuart Roberts, CBS, the staff and crew of *The Late Show*, and our viewers, who make it all possible.